HELLO!

We share what we like.

SCHOLASTIC

LITERACY PLACE®

Copyright acknowledgments and credits appear on page 88, which constitutes an extension of this copyright page.

Copyright © 1996 by Scholastic Inc.   All rights reserved.   Printed in the U.S.A.
                                           ISBN 0-590-56633-4
        5 6 7 8 9 10   23   02 01 00 99 98 97

Stop by
a Writer's Home

We share
what we like.

The chicken koop
where Sundays
dinner chicken
spent it's last
days.

The shed full
of old stuff.
The outhouse
(~~toilet~~) down
beyond the
shed. OK now
but later in
the dark you
wouldn't want
to go.

The smoke house
full of good
meat smells

The pear t
where th
turkeys

Hello!

We share what we like.

Trade Books

The following books accompany this *Hello!* SourceBook.

Realistic Fiction

My Friends
by Taro Gomi

Pattern Story

School Bus
by Donald Crews

Nonfiction

All About You
by Catherine and Laurence Anholt

What Do You Like?
Michael Grejniec

I like the rainbow.

I like the rainbow, too.

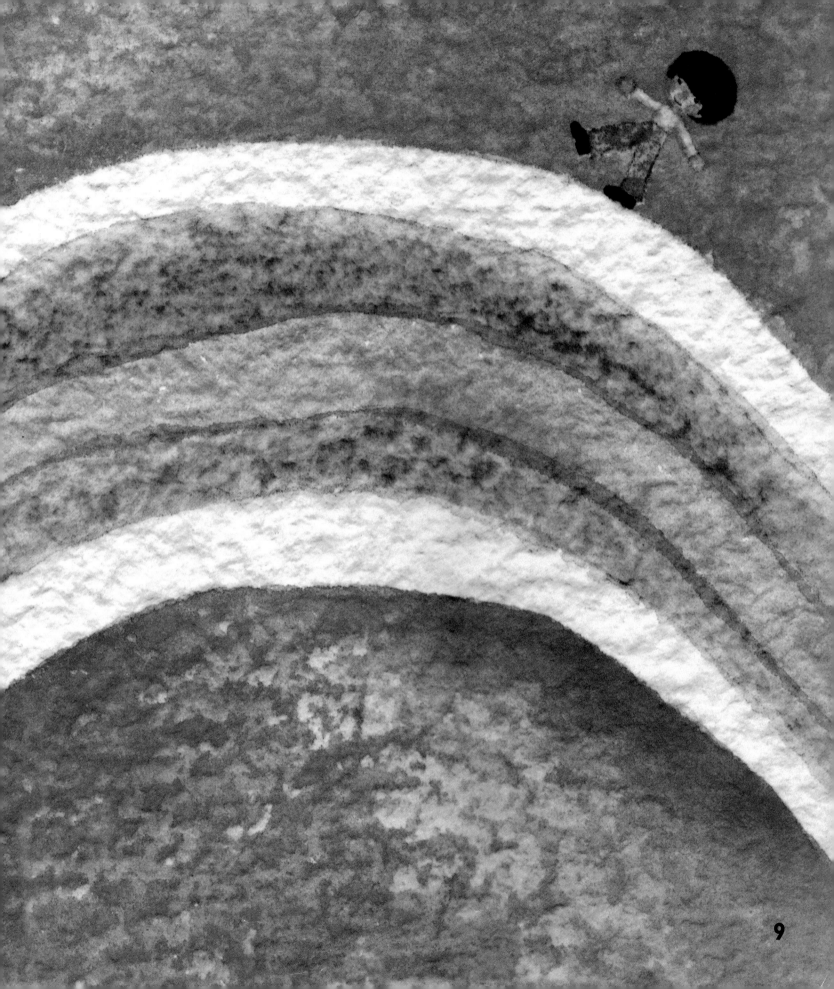

I like to play.

I like to play, too.

I like my cat.

I like my cat, too.

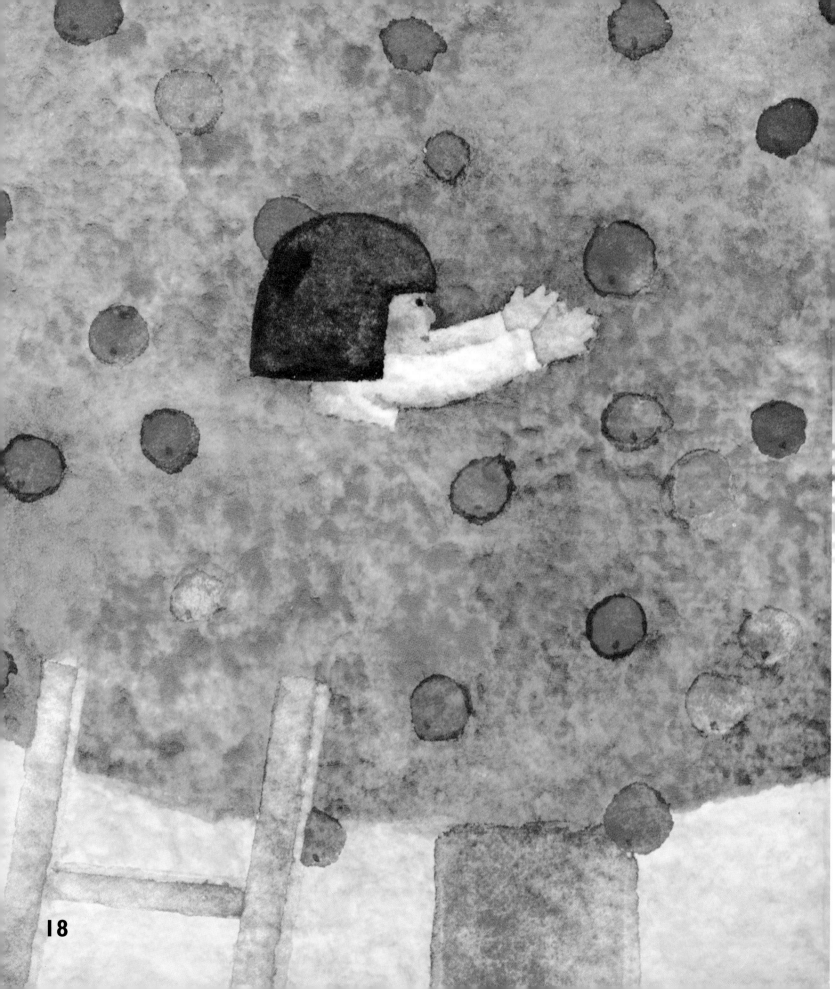

18

I like fruit.

I like fruit, too.

I like music.

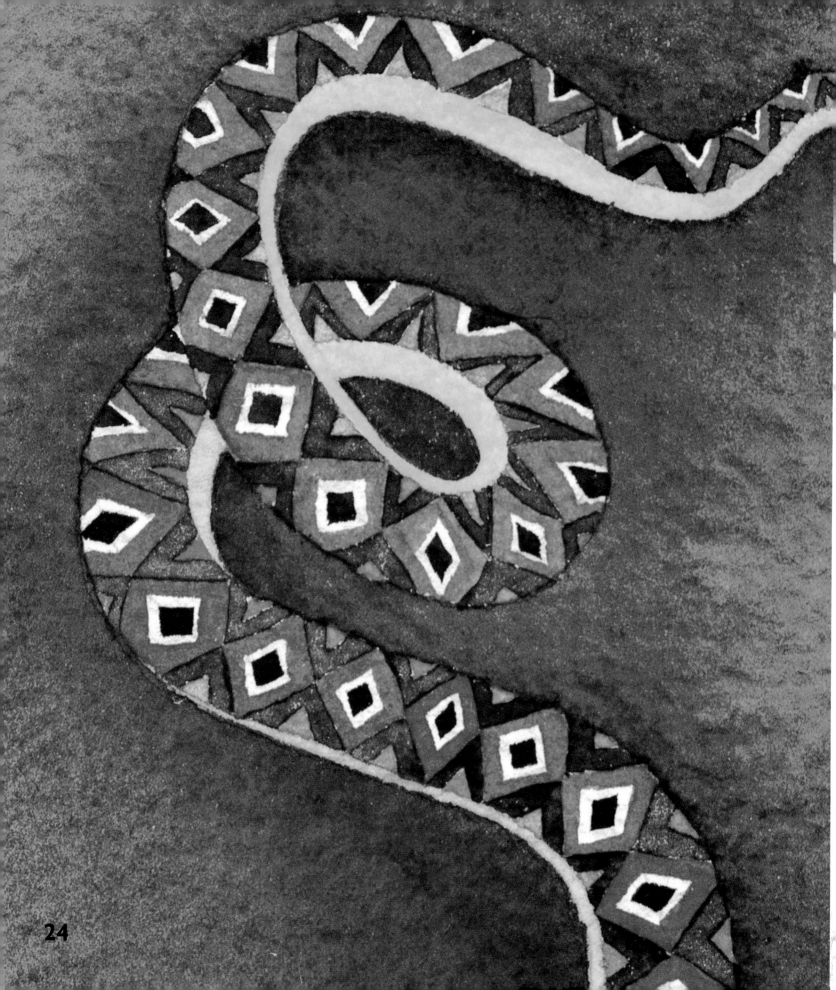

24

I like music, too.

I like to fly.

I like to fly, too.

I love my mother.
I love my mother, too.

What do you like?
What do you love?

📖 Read Together!

Donald Crews

Author

Donald Crews writes books for children. He writes about things he likes and knows about.

He uses old pictures to help him remember when he was a boy.

This is the story he wrote about his summer trip to Florida.

34

Donald Crews
also draws
the pictures
to go with
his stories.

Bo and Peter

Written by Betsy Franco

Illustrated by Stacey Schuett

SCHOLASTIC

AWARD WINNING

Illustrator

Bo and Peter are best friends.

They like to whistle,

shoot baskets,

fly kites,

splash in the water,

eat lunch together,

read books,

play ball,

trade baseball cards,

draw dinosaurs,

and sing songs.

They are always best friends.

Piggy-Back

by Langston Hughes
illustration by Bradford Brown

Read Together!

My daddy rides me
    piggy-back.
My mama rides me, too.
But grandma says her
    poor old back
Has had enough to do.

SOURCE

SESAME STREET MAGAZINE

Magazine

My hair is dark and straight.

My hair is dark and curly.

Read Together!

We're Friends Together!

Friends can be alike.

Friends can be different, too.

Read what these pals have to say.

How are the friends different?

How are they the same?

When I grow up, I want to be a doctor.

When I grow up, I want to be a fire fighter.

I'm happy when Anais reads to me.

I'm happy when I read to Ashley.

We're having fun together! And we love being friends!

53

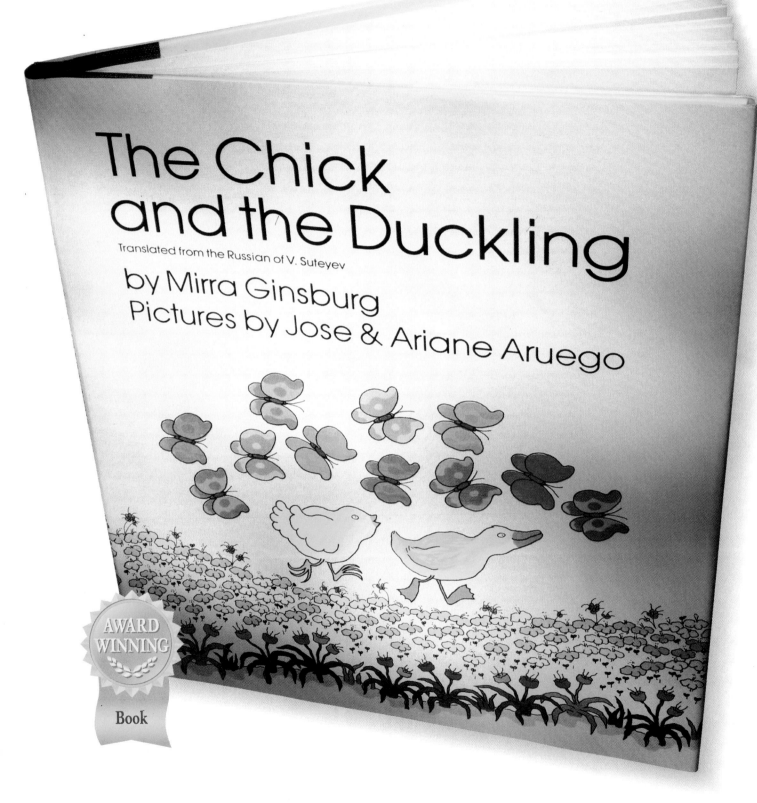

The Chick and the Duckling

Translated from the Russian of V. Suteyev

by Mirra Ginsburg
Pictures by Jose & Ariane Aruego

AWARD WINNING

Book

A Duckling came out
of the shell.

"I am out!" he said.

55

"Me too," said the Chick.

"I am taking a walk,"
said the Duckling.

"Me too,"
said the Chick.

"I am digging a hole,"
said the Duckling.

61

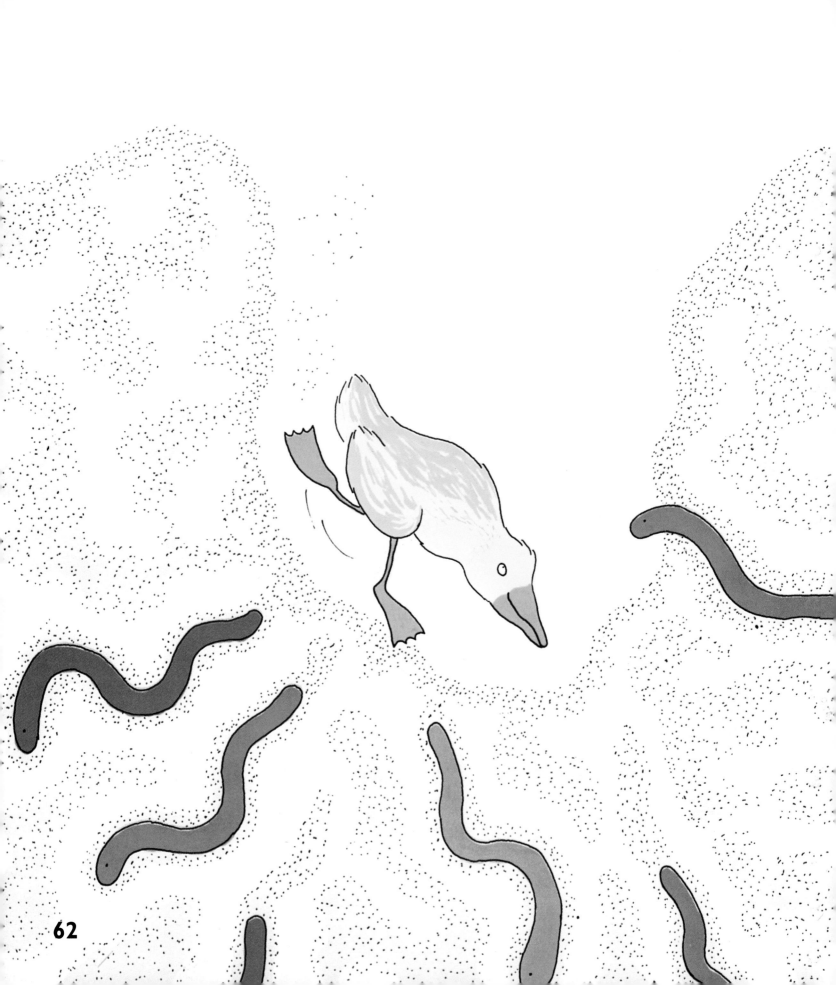

"Me too,"
said the Chick.

"I found a worm,"
said the Duckling.

"Me too,"
said the Chick.

"I caught
a butterfly,"
said the
Duckling.

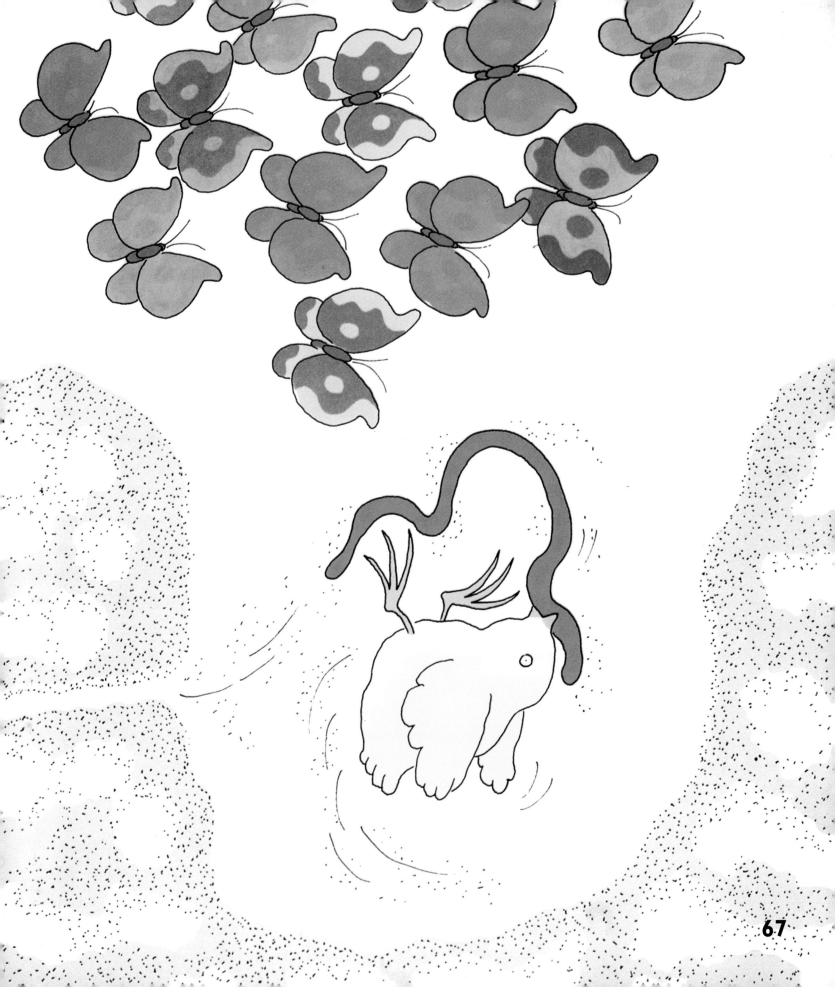

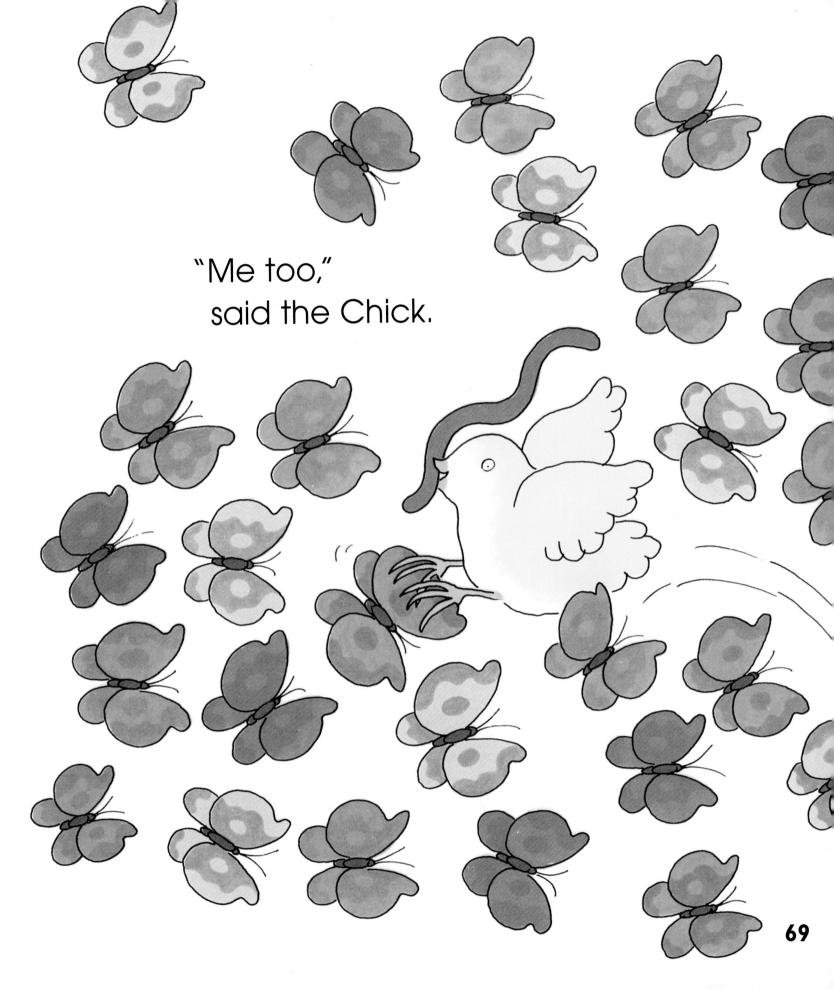

"Me too,"
said the Chick.

"I am going for a swim,"
said the Duckling.

"Me too,"
said the Chick.

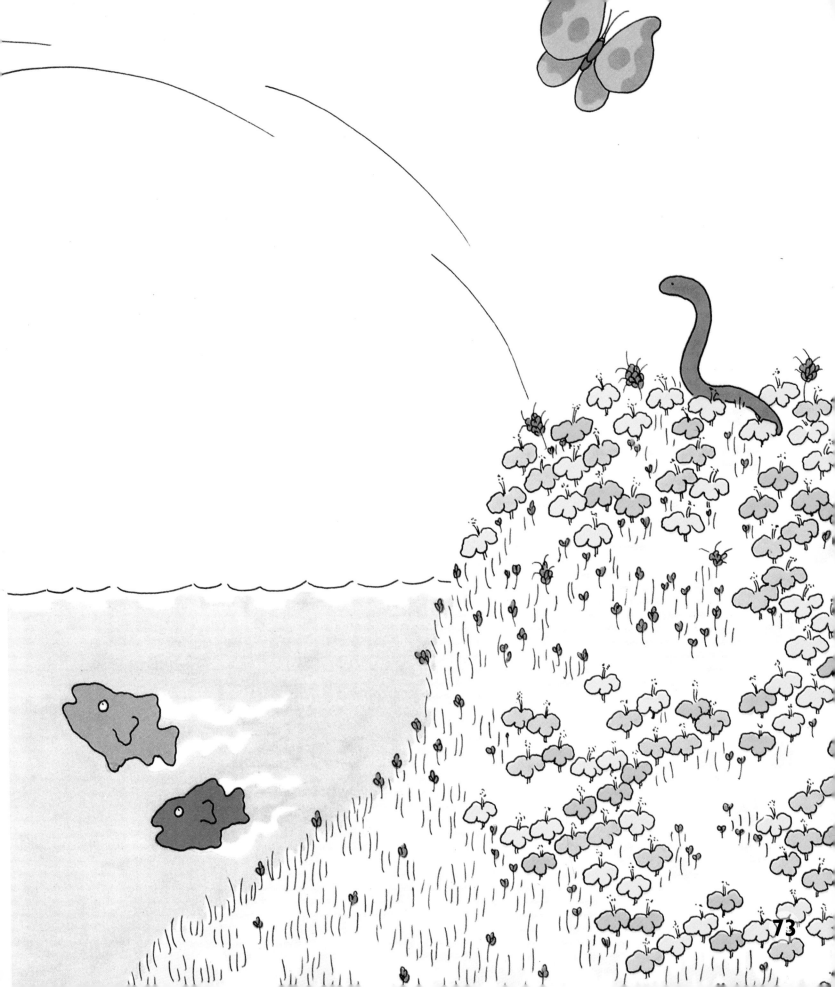

73

"I am swimming,"
said the Duckling.

"Me too!"
cried the Chick.

The Duckling pulled
the Chick out.

"I'm going for another swim,"
said the Duckling.

"Not me,"
said the Chick.

from

📖 Read Together!

Now We Are Six

by A. A. Milne
illustrated by Ernest H. Shepard

The End

When I was One,
I had just begun.

When I was Two,
I was nearly new.

When I was Three,
I was hardly Me.

When I was Four,
I was not much more.

When I was Five,
I was just alive.

But now I am Six, I'm as clever as clever.
So I think I'll be six now for ever and ever.

Glossary

butterfly

fruit

butterfly
a kind of insect that has large wings

That **butterfly** has wings with bright colors.

dinosaur
a kind of animal that lived millions of years ago

The word **dinosaur** comes from the Greek words that mean "terrible lizard."

fruit
the part of a plant that holds the seeds and is often sweet and juicy

Did you know a tomato is a **fruit**?

kites
toys that
fly in the
air at the
end of long
strings
It's hard to fly
kites without
a windy day.

rainbow
a band of colors that form
a wide bow shape across
the sky
A **rainbow** is made from
light passing through
water or mist.

worm
a kind of creeping animal
that has no backbone and
no legs
A **worm** crawls and wiggles.

rainbow

worm

85

Authors and Illustrators

Mirra Ginsburg pages 54-82

Mirra Ginsburg has loved folk tales ever since she was very young. When she was a child in Russia, she saw ducks and chicks in people's yards. "It was almost like living in a folk tale," she says. Some other books by Mirra Ginsburg are *Three Rolls and a Doughnut* and *What Kind of Bird Is That?*

Langston Hughes page 51

Langston Hughes is remembered as one of America's finest poets. When he was little, he lived with his grandmother. She told him long, wonderful stories. When he grew up, he discovered that he was also a great storyteller! His poems and stories have won many prizes.

Read Together!

A. A. Milne page 83

Alan Alexander Milne never forgot what it feels like to be six years old. He even called one of his most famous books *Now We Are Six!* His books of poems and his stories about Winnie-the-Pooh are full of funny characters, playful words, and silly events.

Stacey Schuett pages 36-50

Stacey Schuett says that riding a horse helped her become an artist. Riding gave her time to daydream and use her imagination. Now she uses what she sees, remembers, and imagines in her paintings. *If You Want to Find Golden* by Eileen Spinelli and *Is It Dark? Is It Light?* by Mary Lankford have pictures by Stacey Schuett.

Acknowledgments

Grateful acknowledgment is made to the following sources for permission to reprint from previously published material. The publisher has made diligent efforts to trace the ownership of all copyrighted material in this volume and believes that all necessary permissions have been secured. If any errors or omissions have inadvertently been made, proper corrections will gladly be made in future editions.

Cover: Vincent Andriani.

Interior: "What Do You Like?" from WHAT DO YOU LIKE? by Michael Grejniec. Copyright © 1992 by Michael Grejniec. Reprinted by arrangement with North-South Books Inc., New York. All rights reserved.

"Bo and Peter" from BO AND PETER by Betsy Franco, illustrated by Stacey Schuett. Copyright © 1994 by Scholastic Inc.

"Piggy-Back" from THE LANGSTON HUGHES READER by Langston Hughes. Copyright © 1958 by Langston Hughes, copyright renewed 1986 by George Houston Bass. Reprinted by permission of Harold Ober Associates.

"We're Friends Together!" from *Sesame Street Magazine*, October 1991. Copyright © 1991 Children's Television Workshop, New York, NY. All rights reserved.

"The Chick and the Duckling" from THE CHICK AND THE DUCKLING by Mirra Ginsburg, illustrations by Jose Aruego and Ariane Dewey. Text copyright © 1972 by Mirra Ginsburg. Illustrations copyright © 1972 by Jose Aruego and Ariane Dewey. This edition is reprinted by arrangement with Simon & Schuster Books for Young Readers, Simon & Schuster Children's Publishing Division.

"The End" and cover from NOW WE ARE SIX by A. A. Milne, illustrated by E. H. Shepard. Copyright © 1927 by E. P. Dutton, copyright renewed 1955 by A. A. Milne. Used by permission of Dutton Children's Books, a division of Penguin Books USA Inc.

Cover from ALL ABOUT YOU by Catherine and Laurence Anholt, illustration copyright © 1991 by Catherine and Laurence Anholt. Published by Viking Penguin, a division of Penguin Books USA Inc.

Cover from MY FRIENDS by Taro Gomi. Illustration copyright © 1989 by Taro Gomi. English text copyright © 1990 by Chronicle Books. Published by Chronicle Books.

Cover from SCHOOL BUS by Donald Crews. Illustration copyright © 1984 by Donald Crews. Published by Puffin Books, a division of Penguin Books USA Inc.

Photography and Illustration Credits

Selection Opener Photographs by David S. Waitz Photography/Alleycat Design, Inc.

Photos: p. 2 bl: © Donald Crews. pp. 2-3 cl: © Halley Ganges for Scholastic Inc. p. 3 br: © Halley Ganges for Scholastic Inc. p. 34 bl: © Halley Ganges for Scholastic Inc.; tl: © Donald Crews. pp. 34-35 br: © Halley Ganges for Scholastic Inc. p. 84 bl: © Haroldo Castro/FPG International Corp.; tl: © Gail Shumway/FPG International Corp. p. 85 tl: © Phil Jason/Tony Stone Worldwide; br: © David M. Dennis/Tom Stack & Assoc.; bl: © Telegraph Colour Library/ FPG International Corp. p. 86 br: © AP/Wide World Photo. p. 87 A. A. Milne; bl: © Culver Pictures Inc.; br: Stacey Schuett: © Courtesy of Stacey Schuett.

Illustrations: pp. 2-3: Jackie Snider; pp. 36-50: Stacey Schuett; p. 51: Bradford Brown.